Cookbook
& Recipe Cards

Publications International, Ltd.

Louis Weber, CEO
Publications International, Ltd.
7373 North Cicero Avenue
Lincolnwood, IL 60712

Special thanks to the Campbell's Kitchen and Catherine Marschean-Spivak, Group Manager, and Jane M. Freiman, Group Manager.

Pictured on the front cover (clockwise from top left): Skillet Vegetable Lasagna *(page 48)*, Slow Cooker Savory Pot Roast *(page 78)*, Creamy Chicken Tortilla Soup *(page 68)*, and Creamy Chicken Florentine *(page 40)*.

Pictured on the back cover: Slow Cooker Tuscan Beef Stew *(page 76)*.

ISBN 13: 978-1-60553-727-6
ISBN 10: 1-60553-727-6

Library of Congress Control Number: 2010924384

Manufactured in China.

8 7 6 5 4 3 2 1

Microwave Cooking: Microwave ovens vary in wattage. Use the cooking times as guidelines and check for doneness before adding more time.

Preparation/Cooking Times: Preparation times are based on the approximate amount of time required to assemble the recipe before cooking, baking, chilling or serving. These times include preparation steps such as measuring, chopping and mixing. The fact that some preparations and cooking can be done simultaneously is taken into account. Preparation of optional ingredients and serving suggestions is not included.

Campbell's

Recipes to Share

Every cook loves to impress their guests with a delicious dish—and there's no better complement than being asked for a copy of the recipe. **Campbell's®** *Cookbook & Recipe Cards* is the perfect resource for preparing your favorite dish, then sharing the recipe with your family and friends.

Forty-eight tasty and satisfying recipes await you, each with step-by-step instructions and a mouthwatering photo of the final dish. And for each recipe, you'll also find a recipe card to tear out and share with others.

Why not impress your guests with a classic family favorite like Best-Ever Meatloaf or Easy Chicken & Cheese Enchiladas? Or, give a comforting one-dish Hearty Sausage & Rice Casserole a try. Your next dinner party will be a hit with Melt-in-Your Mouth Short Ribs and Oven Baked Risotto on the side. And, of course, no holiday is complete without Green Bean Casserole.

You'll find recipes for every day and special days just waiting for you and your family and friends to enjoy.

contents

Campbell's

Recipe Cards

family favorite dishes

Chicken & Broccoli Alfredo

MAKES 4 SERVINGS | PREP TIME: 10 minutes | COOK TIME: 20 minutes

- ½ of a 1-pound package linguine
- 1 cup fresh **or** frozen broccoli flowerets
- 2 tablespoons butter
- 1 pound skinless, boneless chicken breasts, cut into 1½-inch pieces
- 1 can (10¾ ounces) Campbell's® Condensed Cream of Mushroom Soup (Regular **or** 98% Fat Free)
- ½ cup milk
- ½ cup grated Parmesan cheese
- ¼ teaspoon ground black pepper

1. Prepare the linguine according to the package directions in a 3-quart saucepan. Add the broccoli during the last 4 minutes of cooking. Drain the linguine mixture well in a colander.

2. Heat the butter in a 10-inch skillet over medium-high heat. Add the chicken and cook until it's well browned, stirring often.

3. Stir the soup, milk, cheese, black pepper and linguine mixture in the skillet. Cook until the mixture is hot and bubbling, stirring occasionally. Serve with additional Parmesan cheese.

Kitchen Tip

You can substitute spaghetti or fettuccine for the linguine in this recipe.

Best-Ever Meatloaf

MAKES 8 SERVINGS

PREP TIME: 10 minutes | BAKE TIME: 1 hour, 15 minutes | COOK TIME: 5 minutes

- **1 can (10¾ ounces) Campbell's® Condensed Cream of Mushroom Soup (Regular *or* 98% Fat Free)**
- **1 small onion, finely chopped (about ¼ cup)**
- **1 egg, beaten**
- **2 pounds ground beef**
- **½ cup dry bread crumbs**
- **½ cup water**

1. Thoroughly mix ½ **cup** soup, onion, egg, beef and bread crumbs in a large bowl. Place the mixture into a 13×9×2-inch baking pan and firmly shape into an 8×4-inch loaf.

2. Bake at 350°F. for 1 hour 15 minutes or until the meatloaf is cooked through.

3. Heat **2 tablespoons** pan drippings, remaining soup and water in a 1-quart saucepan over medium heat until the mixture is hot and bubbling. Serve the sauce with the meatloaf.

Meatloaf Wellington: Prepare as above but bake loaf only 1 hour. Spoon off fat. Separate **1 package** (8 ounces) refrigerated crescent rolls. Place triangles crosswise over top and down sides of meatloaf, overlapping slightly. Bake 15 minutes more until golden.

Frosted Meatloaf: Prepare as above but bake loaf only 1 hour. Spoon off fat. Spread **3 cups** hot, seasoned mashed potatoes over loaf; sprinkle with ½ **cup** shredded Cheddar cheese. Bake 15 to 30 minutes more until meat is done.

Garlic Mashed Potatoes & Beef Bake

MAKES 4 SERVINGS | PREP TIME: 15 minutes | BAKE TIME: 20 minutes

- **1 pound ground beef**
- **1 can (10¾ ounces) Campbell's® Condensed Cream of Mushroom with Roasted Garlic Soup**
- **1 tablespoon Worcestershire sauce**
- **1 bag (16 ounces) frozen vegetable combination (broccoli, cauliflower, carrots), thawed**
- **2 cups water**
- **3 tablespoons butter**
- **¾ cup milk**
- **2 cups instant mashed potato flakes**

1. Heat the oven to 400°F. Cook the beef in a 10-inch skillet over medium-high heat until it's well browned, stirring often to separate meat. Pour off any fat.

2. Stir the beef, ½ **can** soup, Worcestershire and vegetables in a 2-quart shallow baking dish.

3. Heat the water, butter and remaining soup in a 3-quart saucepan over medium heat to a boil. Remove the saucepan from the heat. Stir in the milk. Stir in the potatoes. Spoon the potatoes over the beef mixture.

4. Bake for 20 minutes or until the potatoes are lightly browned.

Kitchen Tip

You can use your favorite frozen vegetable combination in this recipe.

Sloppy Joe Casserole

MAKES 5 SERVINGS | PREP TIME: 15 minutes | BAKE TIME: 15 minutes

- **1 pound ground beef**
- **1 can (10¾ ounces) Campbell's® Condensed Tomato Soup (Regular *or* Healthy Request®)**
- **¼ cup water**
- **1 teaspoon Worcestershire sauce**
- **⅛ teaspoon ground black pepper**
- **1 package (7.5 ounces) refrigerated biscuits (10 biscuits)**
- **½ cup shredded Cheddar cheese**

1. Heat the oven to 400°F.

2. Cook the beef in a 10-inch skillet over medium-high heat until it's well browned, stirring often to separate meat. Pour off any fat.

3. Stir the soup, water, Worcestershire and black pepper in the skillet and heat to a boil. Spoon the beef mixture into a 1½-quart casserole. Arrange the biscuits around the inside edge of the casserole.

4. Bake for 15 minutes or until the biscuits are golden brown. Sprinkle the cheese over the beef mixture.

Kitchen Tip

Sharp or mild Cheddar cheese will work in this recipe.

Skillet Fiesta Chicken & Rice

MAKES 4 SERVINGS | PREP TIME: 5 minutes | COOK TIME: 20 minutes

- **1 tablespoon vegetable oil**
- **4 skinless, boneless chicken breast halves**
- **1 can (10¾ ounces) Campbell's® Condensed Tomato Soup (Regular *or* Healthy Request®)**
- **1⅓ cups water**
- **1 teaspoon chili powder**
- **1½ cups *uncooked* instant white rice**
- **¼ cup shredded Cheddar cheese**

1. Heat the oil in a 10-inch skillet over medium-high heat. Add the chicken and cook for 10 minutes or until it's well browned on both sides. Remove the chicken from the skillet.

2. Stir the soup, water and chili powder in the skillet and heat to a boil.

3. Stir in the rice. Place the chicken on the rice mixture. Sprinkle the chicken with additional chili powder and the cheese. Reduce the heat to low. Cover and cook for 5 minutes or until the chicken is cooked through and the rice is tender. Stir the rice mixture before serving.

Kitchen Tip

Try Mexican-blend shredded cheese instead of the Cheddar if you like.

Creamy Pork Marsala with Fettuccine

MAKES 4 SERVINGS | PREP TIME: 5 minutes | COOK TIME: 25 minutes

- **1 tablespoon olive oil**
- **4 boneless pork chops, ¾-inch thick**
- **1 cup sliced mushrooms (about 3 ounces)**
- **1 clove garlic, minced**
- **1 can (10¾ ounces) Campbell's® Condensed Cream of Mushroom Soup (Regular *or* 98% Fat Free)**
- **½ cup milk**
- **2 tablespoons dry Marsala wine**
- **8 ounces spinach fettuccine, cooked and drained**

1. Heat the oil in a 10-inch skillet over medium-high heat. Add the pork and cook until it's well browned on both sides.

2. Reduce the heat to medium. Add the mushrooms and garlic to the skillet and cook until the mushrooms are tender.

3. Stir the soup, milk and wine in the skillet and heat to a boil. Reduce the heat to low. Cover and cook for 5 minutes or until the pork is cooked through. Serve the pork and sauce with the pasta.

Kitchen Tip

Marsalas can range from dry to sweet, so be sure to use a dry one for this recipe.

Simple Salisbury Steaks

MAKES 4 SERVINGS | PREP TIME: 15 minutes | COOK TIME: 25 minutes

1 can (10¾ ounces) Campbell's® Condensed Cream of Mushroom
   Soup (Regular *or* 98% Fat Free)
1 pound ground beef
⅓ cup dry bread crumbs
1 small onion, finely chopped (about ¼ cup)
1 egg, beaten
1 tablespoon vegetable oil
1½ cups sliced mushrooms (about 4 ounces)

1. Thoroughly mix ¼ **cup** soup, beef, bread crumbs, onion and egg in a large bowl. Shape **firmly** into **4** (½-inch-thick) patties.

2. Heat the oil in a 10-inch skillet over medium-high heat. Add the patties and cook until they're well browned on both sides. Pour off any fat.

3. Add the remaining soup and mushrooms to the skillet and heat to a boil. Reduce the heat to low. Cover and cook for 10 minutes or until the patties are cooked through.

French Onion Burgers

MAKES 4 SERVINGS | PREP TIME: 5 minutes | COOK TIME: 20 minutes

1 pound ground beef
1 can (10½ ounces) Campbell's® Condensed French Onion Soup
4 slices Swiss cheese
4 round hard rolls, split

1. Shape the beef into **4** (½-inch-thick) burgers.

2. Heat a 10-inch skillet over medium-high heat. Add the burgers and cook until they're well browned on both sides. Remove the burgers from the skillet. Pour off any fat.

3. Stir the soup in the skillet and heat to a boil. Return the burgers to the skillet. Reduce the heat to low. Cover and cook for 5 minutes or until the burgers are cooked through. Top the burgers with the cheese and cook until the cheese is melted. Serve the burgers in the rolls with the soup mixture.

Kitchen Tip

You can also serve these burgers in a bowl atop a mound of hot mashed potatoes, with some of the onion gravy poured over.

Easy Chicken & Cheese Enchiladas

MAKES 6 SERVINGS | PREP TIME: 15 minutes | BAKE TIME: 40 minutes

- **1 can (10¾ ounces) Campbell's® Condensed Cream of Chicken Soup (Regular *or* 98% Fat Free)**
- **½ cup sour cream**
- **1 cup Pace® Picante Sauce**
- **2 teaspoons chili powder**
- **2 cups chopped cooked chicken**
- **½ cup shredded Monterey Jack cheese**
- **6 flour tortillas (6-inch), warmed**
- **1 small tomato, chopped (about ½ cup)**
- **1 green onion, sliced (about 2 tablespoons)**

1. Heat the oven to 350°F. Stir the soup, sour cream, picante sauce and chili powder in a medium bowl.

2. Stir **1 cup** picante sauce mixture, chicken and cheese in a large bowl.

3. Divide the chicken mixture among the tortillas. Roll up the tortillas and place them, seam-side up, in a 2-quart shallow baking dish. Pour the remaining picante sauce mixture over the filled tortillas. Cover the baking dish.

4. Bake for 40 minutes or until the enchiladas are hot and bubbling. Top with the tomato and onion.

Kitchen Tip

*Stir ½ **cup** canned black beans, drained and rinsed, into the chicken mixture before filling the tortillas.*

Creamy Pesto Chicken & Bow Ties

MAKES 4 SERVINGS | PREP TIME: 5 minutes | COOK TIME: 15 minutes

- **2 tablespoons butter**
- **1 pound skinless, boneless chicken breasts, cut into cubes**
- **1 can (10¾ ounces) Campbell's® Cream of Chicken Soup (Regular *or* 98% Fat Free)**
- **½ cup milk**
- **½ cup prepared pesto sauce**
- **3 cups bow tie-shaped pasta (farfalle), cooked and drained**

1. Heat the butter in a 10-inch skillet over medium-high heat. Add the chicken and cook until it's well browned, stirring often.

2. Stir the soup, milk and pesto sauce into the skillet. Heat to a boil. Reduce the heat to low. Cover and cook over low for 5 minutes or until the chicken is cooked through. Stir in the pasta. Cook until it's hot.

Chicken Quesadillas & Fiesta Rice

MAKES 10 QUESADILLAS | PREP TIME: 5 minutes | COOK TIME: 15 minutes

Vegetable cooking spray
 1 **pound skinless, boneless chicken breasts, cubed**
 1 **can (10¾ ounces) Campbell's® Condensed Cheddar Cheese Soup**
 ½ **cup Pace® Picante Sauce**
 10 **flour tortillas (8-inch)**
Fiesta Rice (recipe follows)

1. Heat the oven to 425°F.

2. Spray a 10-inch skillet with cooking spray. Heat over medium-high heat for 1 minute. Add the chicken and cook until it's well browned, stirring often.

3. Stir the soup and salsa into the skillet. Cook until the mixture is hot and bubbling, stirring occasionally.

4. Put the tortillas on 2 baking sheets. Top **half** of each tortilla with **about** ⅓ **cup** soup mixture to within ½ inch of the edge. Moisten the edge of each tortilla with water. Fold over and press edges together to seal.

5. Bake for 5 minutes or until the filling is hot. Serve with *Fiesta Rice*.

Fiesta Rice: Heat **1 can** Campbell's® Condensed Chicken Broth, ½ **cup** water and ½ **cup** Pace® Picante Sauce in a 2-quart saucepan over high heat to a boil. Stir in **2 cups uncooked** instant white rice. Cover and remove from the heat. Let stand 5 minutes, and then fluff the rice with a fork.

Tasty 2-Step Chicken

MAKES 6 SERVINGS | PREP TIME: 5 minutes | COOK TIME: 20 minutes

1 **tablespoon vegetable oil**
4 **skinless, boneless chicken breast halves**
1 **can (10¾ ounces) Campbell's® Condensed Cream of Mushroom Soup (Regular *or* 98% Fat Free)**
½ **cup water**

1. Heat the oil in a 10-inch skillet over medium-high heat. Add the chicken and cook for 10 minutes or until it's browned. Set the chicken aside. Pour off any fat.

2. Stir the soup and water into the skillet. Heat to a boil. Return the chicken to the skillet and reduce the heat to low. Cover and cook for 5 minutes or until the chicken is cooked through.

Paprika Chicken with Sour Cream Gravy

MAKES 4 SERVINGS | PREP TIME: 10 minutes | COOK TIME: 20 minutes

- ½ **cup all-purpose flour**
- 2 **teaspoons paprika**
- 1 **teaspoon garlic powder**
- 1 **teaspoon ground black pepper**
- 1 **teaspoon ground red pepper**
- 4 **skinless, boneless chicken breast halves**
- ¼ **cup butter**
- 1 **can (10¾ ounces) Campbell's® Condensed Cream of Chicken Soup (Regular *or* 98% Fat Free)**
- 2 **green onions, sliced (about ¼ cup)**
- 1 **container (8 ounces) sour cream**

1. Stir the flour, paprika, garlic powder, black pepper and red pepper on a plate. Coat the chicken with the paprika mixture.

2. Heat the butter in a 10-inch skillet over medium-high heat. Cook the chicken for 10 minutes or until it's well browned on both sides. Remove the chicken from the skillet.

3. Stir the soup and green onions in the skillet and heat to a boil. Return the chicken to the skillet. Reduce the heat to low. Cover and cook for 5 minutes or until the chicken is cooked through. Stir in the sour cream.

Kitchen Tip

Serve with a rice blend, steamed cut green beans and carrot slices.

Cheeseburger Pasta

MAKES 5 SERVINGS | PREP TIME: 5 minutes | COOK TIME: 20 minutes

1 **pound ground beef**
1 **can (10¾ ounces) Campbell's® Condensed Cheddar Cheese Soup**
1 **can (10¾ ounces) Campbell's® Condensed Tomato Soup (Regular or Healthy Request®)**
1½ **cups water**
2 **cups *uncooked* medium shell-shaped pasta**

1. Cook the beef in a 10-inch skillet over medium-high heat until it's well browned, stirring often to separate meat. Pour off any fat.

2. Stir the soups, water and pasta in the skillet and heat to a boil. Reduce the heat to medium. Cook for 10 minutes or until the pasta is tender, stirring often.

casseroles & one-dish meals

Beefy Pasta Skillet

| MAKES 4 SERVINGS | PREP TIME: 5 minutes | COOK TIME: 15 minutes |

- **1 pound ground beef**
- **1 medium onion, chopped (about ½ cup)**
- **1 can (10¾ ounces) Campbell's® Condensed Tomato Soup (Regular *or* Healthy Request®)**
- **¼ cup water**
- **1 tablespoon Worcestershire sauce**
- **½ cup shredded Cheddar cheese**
- **2 cups cooked corkscrew-shaped pasta (rotini) *or* elbow pasta**

1. Cook the beef and onion in a 10-inch skillet over medium-high heat until the beef is well browned, stirring often to separate the meat. Pour off any fat.

2. Stir the soup, water, Worcestershire, cheese and pasta in the skillet and cook until the mixture is hot and bubbling.

Easy Chicken & Biscuits

MAKES 5 SERVINGS | PREP TIME: 10 minutes | BAKE TIME: 30 minutes

1 can (10¾ ounces) Campbell's® Condensed Cream of Celery Soup (Regular *or* 98% Fat Free)

1 can (10¾ ounces) Campbell's® Condensed Cream of Potato Soup

1 cup milk

¼ teaspoon dried thyme leaves, crushed

¼ teaspoon ground black pepper

4 cups cooked cut-up vegetables*

2 cups cubed cooked chicken

1 package (about 7 ounces) refrigerated buttermilk biscuits (10)

Use a combination of broccoli flowerets, cauliflower flowerets and carrots.

1. Stir the soups, milk, thyme, black pepper, vegetables and chicken in a 13×9×2-inch shallow baking dish.

2. Bake at 400°F. for 15 minutes. Stir.

3. Cut each biscuit into quarters. Arrange cut biscuits over the chicken mixture.

4. Bake for 15 minutes more or until the biscuits are golden.

Tuscan Turkey & Beans

MAKES 4 SERVINGS | PREP TIME: 10 minutes | COOK TIME: 20 minutes

- 2 tablespoons olive *or* vegetable oil
- 4 turkey breast cutlets *or* slices (about 1 pound)
- 1 medium onion, chopped (about ½ cup)
- 2 cloves garlic, minced
- 1½ teaspoons dried Italian seasoning, crushed
- 1 can (about 14.5 ounces) diced tomatoes, undrained
- 1½ cups packed chopped fresh spinach leaves
- 1 can (10¾ ounces) Campbell's® Condensed Cream of Celery Soup (Regular *or* 98% Fat Free)
- ¼ teaspoon ground black pepper
- 1 can (about 16 ounces) white kidney beans (cannellini), rinsed and drained

  Grated *or* shredded Parmesan cheese

1. Heat **1 tablespoon** of the oil in a large skillet over medium-high heat. Add the turkey in 2 batches and cook for 3 minutes or until it's lightly browned on both sides. Remove the turkey from the skillet and set aside.

2. Add the remaining oil to the skillet and heat over medium heat. Add the onion, garlic and Italian seasoning and cook until the onion is tender-crisp, stirring often.

3. Add the tomatoes and the spinach and cook just until the spinach is wilted, stirring occasionally. Add the soup, black pepper and beans. Heat to a boil. Return the turkey to the skillet. Reduce the heat to low. Cover and cook for 5 minutes or until the turkey is cooked through. Sprinkle with the cheese.

Cheesy Chicken & Rice Casserole

MAKES 4 SERVINGS
PREP TIME: 15 minutes | BAKE TIME: 50 minutes | STAND TIME: 10 minutes

1 can (10¾ ounces) Campbell's® Condensed Cream of Chicken Soup (Regular *or* 98% Fat Free)

1⅓ cups water

¾ cup *uncooked* regular long-grain white rice

½ teaspoon onion powder

¼ teaspoon ground black pepper

2 cups frozen mixed vegetables

4 skinless, boneless chicken breast halves

½ cup shredded Cheddar cheese

1. Heat the oven to 375°F. Stir the soup, water, rice, onion powder, black pepper and vegetables in a 2-quart shallow baking dish.

2. Top with the chicken. Season the chicken as desired. Cover the baking dish.

3. Bake for 50 minutes or until the chicken is cooked through and the rice is tender. Top with the cheese. Let the casserole stand for 10 minutes. Stir the rice before serving.

Kitchen Tip

*To try it Alfredo, substitute broccoli flowerets for the vegetables and substitute ¼ **cup** grated Parmesan for the Cheddar cheese. Add **2 tablespoons** Parmesan cheese with the soup. Sprinkle the chicken with the remaining Parmesan cheese.*

Trim It Down: Use **Campbell's®** 98% Fat Free Condensed Cream of Chicken Soup instead of regular soup and use low-fat cheese instead of regular cheese.

Mexican: In place of onion powder and pepper use **1 teaspoon** chili powder. Substitute Mexican cheese blend for Cheddar.

Italian: In place of onion powder and pepper use **1 teaspoon** Italian seasoning, crushed. Substitute ⅓ **cup** shredded Parmesan for Cheddar.

Creamy Chicken Florentine

MAKES 4 SERVINGS
PREP TIME: 15 minutes | BAKE TIME: 40 minutes | STAND TIME: 5 minutes

**1 can (10¾ ounces) Campbell's® Condensed Cream of Chicken
   Soup (Regular _or_ 98% Fat Free)**
1½ cups water
 **½ of a 20-ounce bag frozen cut-leaf spinach, thawed and well
   drained (about 3½ cups)**
 1 can (about 14.5 ounces) diced tomatoes with Italian herbs
 1 pound skinless, boneless chicken breasts, cut into 1-inch cubes
2½ cups _uncooked_ penne pasta
 ½ cup shredded mozzarella cheese

1. Heat the oven to 375°F. Stir the soup, water, spinach, tomatoes and
chicken in a 3-quart shallow baking dish. Cover the baking dish.

2. Bake for 20 minutes. Cook the pasta according to the package directions
and drain well in a colander. Uncover the baking dish and stir in the pasta.

3. Bake for 20 minutes or until the pasta mixture is hot and bubbling.
Sprinkle with the cheese. Let stand for 5 minutes or until the cheese is
melted.

Tuna & Pasta Cheddar Melt

MAKES 4 SERVINGS | **PREP TIME:** 10 minutes | **COOK TIME:** 15 minutes

1 can (10½ ounces) Campbell's® Condensed Chicken Broth

1 soup can water

½ of a 1-pound package *uncooked* corkscrew-shaped pasta (rotini) (about 3 cups)

1 can (10¾ ounces) Campbell's® Condensed Cream of Mushroom Soup (Regular *or* 98% Fat Free)

1 cup milk

1 can (about 6 ounces) tuna, drained and flaked

1 cup shredded Cheddar cheese (about 4 ounces)

2 tablespoons Italian-seasoned dry bread crumbs

2 teaspoons butter or margarine, melted

1. Heat the broth and the water to a boil over medium-high heat in a large skillet. Add the pasta and cook until it's just tender, stirring often. Do not drain.

2. Stir the soup, milk and tuna in the skillet. Top with the cheese. Mix the bread crumbs with the butter. Sprinkle on top. Heat through.

Hearty Sausage & Rice Casserole

MAKES 6 SERVINGS | PREP TIME: 30 minutes | BAKE TIME: 1 hour

- 1 **pound bulk pork sausage**
- 1 **package (8 ounces) sliced mushrooms**
- 2 **stalks celery, coarsely chopped (about 1 cup)**
- 1 **large red pepper, coarsely chopped (about 1 cup)**
- 1 **large onion, coarsely chopped (about 1 cup)**
- 1 **teaspoon dried thyme leaves, crushed**
- ½ **teaspoon dried marjoram leaves, crushed**
- 1 **box (6 ounces) seasoned long-grain and wild rice mix**
- 1¾ **cups Swanson® Chicken Stock**
- 1 **can (10¾ ounces) Campbell's® Condensed Cream of Mushroom Soup (Regular *or* 98% Fat Free)**
- 1 **cup shredded Cheddar cheese (about 4 ounces)**

1. Cook the sausage in a 12-inch skillet over medium-high heat until it's well browned, stirring often to separate meat. Pour off any fat.

2. Add the mushrooms, celery, pepper, onion, thyme, marjoram and seasoning packet from the rice blend to the skillet and cook until the vegetables are tender-crisp.

3. Stir the sausage mixture, stock, soup, rice blend and ½ **cup** cheese in a 3-quart shallow baking dish. Cover the baking dish.

4. Bake at 375°F. for 1 hour or until the sausage is cooked through and the rice is tender. Stir the sausage mixture before serving. Sprinkle with the remaining cheese.

Kitchen Tip

*For an extra-special touch, substitute **1 package** (8 ounces) baby portobello mushrooms, sliced, for the sliced mushrooms.*

Beef Stroganoff

MAKES 4 SERVINGS | PREP TIME: 10 minutes | COOK TIME: 25 minutes

- **1 tablespoon vegetable oil**
- **1 pound boneless beef sirloin steak *or* beef top round steak, ¾-inch thick, cut into thin strips**
- **1 medium onion, chopped (about ½ cup)**
- **1 can (10¾ ounces) Campbell's® Condensed Cream of Mushroom Soup (Regular *or* 98% Fat Free)**
- **½ teaspoon paprika**
- **⅓ cup sour cream *or* plain yogurt**
- **4 cups hot cooked whole wheat *or* regular egg noodles**
  Chopped fresh parsley

1. Heat the oil in a 12-inch nonstick skillet over medium-high heat. Add the beef and cook until it's well browned, stirring often. Remove the beef from the skillet. Pour off any fat.

2. Reduce the heat to medium. Add the onion to the skillet and cook until it's tender.

3. Stir the soup and paprika in the skillet and heat to a boil. Stir in the sour cream. Return the beef to the skillet and cook until the mixture is hot and bubbling. Serve the beef mixture over the noodles. Sprinkle with the parsley.

Skillet Vegetable Lasagna

MAKES 4 SERVINGS | PREP TIME: 10 minutes | COOK TIME: 15 minutes

1¾ cups Swanson® Vegetable Broth (Regular *or* Certified Organic)

⅔ of a 1-pound package of *uncooked* oven-ready (no-boil) lasagna noodles (about 15)

1 can (10¾ ounces) Campbell's® Condensed Cream of Mushroom Soup (Regular *or* 98% Fat Free)

1 can (about 14.5 ounces) diced tomatoes, undrained

1 package (10 ounces) frozen chopped spinach, thawed and well drained

1 cup ricotta cheese

1 cup shredded mozzarella cheese (about 4 ounces)

1. Heat the broth in a 12-inch skillet over medium-high heat to a boil. Break the noodles into pieces and add to the broth. Reduce the heat to low. Cook for 3 minutes or until the noodles are tender.

2. Stir the soup, tomatoes and spinach in the skillet. Cook for 5 minutes or until the mixture is hot and bubbling.

3. Remove the skillet from the heat. Spoon the ricotta cheese on top and sprinkle with the mozzarella cheese.

Kitchen Tip

*You can try using **4 ounces** mozzarella, cut into very thin slices, instead of the shredded mozzarella.*

Hearty Chicken & Noodle Casserole

MAKES 4 SERVINGS | **PREP TIME:** 15 minutes | **BAKE TIME:** 25 minutes

- **1 can (10¾ ounces) Campbell's® Condensed Cream of Mushroom Soup (Regular *or* 98% Fat Free)**
- **½ cup milk**
- **¼ teaspoon ground black pepper**
- **1 cup frozen mixed vegetables**
- **2 cups cubed cooked chicken**
- **¼ of a 12-ounce package medium egg noodles (about 2 cups), cooked and drained**
- **¼ cup grated Parmesan cheese**
- **½ cup shredded Cheddar cheese**

1. Heat the oven to 400°F. Stir the soup, milk, black pepper, vegetables, chicken, noodles and Parmesan cheese in a 1½-quart casserole.

2. Bake for 25 minutes or until the chicken mixture is hot and bubbling. Stir the chicken mixture. Top with the Cheddar cheese.

Kitchen Tip

*Easy casseroles like this one are a simple way to transform leftovers; cooked chicken, turkey **or** ham will all work in this recipe. Or, substitute **1 can** (12.5 ounces) Swanson® Premium White Chunk Chicken Breast, drained, for the cubed cooked chicken.*

Chicken Broccoli Divan

MAKES 4 SERVINGS	PREP TIME: 10 minutes	BAKE TIME: 20 minutes

- **4 cups cooked broccoli flowerets**
- **1½ cups cubed cooked chicken**
- **1 can (10¾ ounces) Campbell's® Condensed Cream of Chicken Soup (Regular *or* 98% Fat Free)**
- **⅓ cup milk**
- **½ cup shredded Cheddar cheese**
- **2 tablespoons dry bread crumbs**
- **1 tablespoon butter, melted**

1. Heat the oven to 450°F. Place the broccoli and chicken into a 9-inch deep-dish pie plate.

2. Stir the soup and milk in a small bowl. Pour the soup mixture over the broccoli and chicken. Sprinkle with the cheese. Stir the bread crumbs and butter in a small bowl. Sprinkle the bread crumbs over the cheese.

3. Bake for 20 minutes or until the cheese is melted and the bread crumbs are golden brown.

Kitchen Tip

You can use leftover cooked turkey instead of the chicken in this recipe.

One-Dish Chicken & Stuffing Bake

MAKES 6 SERVINGS | **PREP TIME:** 15 minutes | **BAKE TIME:** 30 minutes

- 4 cups Pepperidge Farm® Herb Seasoned Stuffing
- 6 skinless, boneless chicken breast halves
  Paprika
- 1 can (10¾ ounces) Campbell's® Condensed Cream of Mushroom Soup (Regular *or* 98% Fat Free)
- ⅓ cup milk
- 1 tablespoon chopped fresh parsley *or* 1 teaspoon dried parsley flakes

1. Heat the oven to 400°F. Prepare the stuffing according to the package directions.

2. Spoon the stuffing across the center of a 3-quart shallow baking dish. Place the chicken on either side of the stuffing. Sprinkle the chicken with the paprika.

3. Stir the soup, milk and parsley in a small bowl. Pour the soup mixture over the chicken. Cover the baking dish.

4. Bake for 30 minutes or until the chicken is cooked through.

Kitchen Tip

4 cups of any variety of Pepperidge Farm® Stuffing will work in this recipe.

New Orleans Shrimp Toss

| MAKES 4 SERVINGS | PREP TIME: 15 minutes | COOK TIME: 10 minutes |

- **1 pound large shrimp, shelled and deveined**
- **2 tablespoons vegetable oil**
- **2 tablespoons lemon juice**
- **1 tablespoon Worcestershire sauce**
- **1 teaspoon Cajun seasoning**
- **½ cup chopped onion**
- **2 cloves garlic, chopped**
- **1 can Campbell's® Condensed Cream of Chicken with Herbs Soup**
- **½ cup milk**
- **1 teaspoon paprika**
- **2 tablespoons chopped fresh chives (optional)**
- **Cornbread *or* biscuits**

1. Stir the shrimp, **1 tablespoon** oil, lemon juice, Worcestershire and Cajun seasoning in a medium bowl.

2. Heat the remaining oil in a 10-inch skillet over medium heat. Add the onion and garlic and cook until they're tender.

3. Stir the soup, milk and paprika in the skillet. Heat to a boil. Add the shrimp mixture. Reduce the heat to low. Cover and cook for 5 minutes or until the shrimp are done. Garnish with the chives, if desired. Serve with the cornbread.

Beef Taco Skillet

MAKES 4 SERVINGS | **PREP TIME:** 5 minutes | **COOK TIME:** 20 minutes

1 pound ground beef

1 can (10¾ ounces) Campbell's® Condensed Tomato Soup (Regular *or* Healthy Request®)

½ cup salsa

½ cup water

6 flour tortillas (6-inch), cut into 1-inch pieces

½ cup shredded Cheddar cheese

1. Cook the beef in a 10-inch skillet over medium-high heat until it's well browned, stirring often to separate meat. Pour off any fat.

2. Stir the soup, salsa, water and tortillas in the skillet and heat to a boil. Reduce the heat to low. Cook for 5 minutes. Stir the beef mixture. Top with the cheese.

Creamy Pork Sauté

MAKES 4 SERVINGS | **PREP TIME:** 10 minutes | **COOK TIME:** 25 minutes

- 2 tablespoons vegetable oil
- 1 pound boneless pork loin, cut into thin strips
- 2 stalks celery, sliced (about 1 cup)
- 1 medium onion, chopped (about ½ cup)
- ½ teaspoon dried thyme leaves, crushed
- 1 can (10¾ ounces) Campbell's® Condensed Cream of Celery Soup (Regular *or* 98% Fat Free)
- ¼ cup water
  Hot cooked regular long-grain white rice

1. Heat **1 tablespoon** oil in a 10-inch skillet over medium-high heat. Add the pork and cook until it's well browned, stirring often. Remove the pork from the skillet.

2. Heat the remaining oil over medium heat. Add the celery, onion and thyme and cook until the vegetables are tender, stirring often.

3. Stir the soup and water in the skillet and heat to a boil. Return the pork to the skillet. Cook until the pork is cooked through. Serve the pork mixture over the rice.

Tuna Noodle Casserole

MAKES 8 SERVINGS | **PREP TIME:** 10 minutes | **BAKE TIME:** 35 minutes

- 2 cans (10¾ ounces *each*) Campbell's® Condensed Cream of Mushroom Soup (Regular *or* 98% Fat Free)
- 1 cup milk
- 2 cups frozen peas
- 2 cans (about 10 ounces *each*) tuna, drained
- ½ of a 12-ounce package medium egg noodles (about 4 cups), cooked and drained
- 2 tablespoons dry bread crumbs
- 1 tablespoon butter, melted

1. Stir the soup, milk, peas, tuna and noodles in a 3-quart casserole.

2. Bake at 400°F. for 30 minutes or until the tuna mixture is hot and bubbling. Stir the tuna mixture.

3. Stir the bread crumbs and butter in a small bowl. Sprinkle the bread crumb mixture over the tuna mixture. Bake for 5 minutes or until the topping is golden brown.

comforting
slow cooker suppers

Melt-in-Your-Mouth Short Ribs

MAKES 6 SERVINGS | **PREP TIME:** 10 minutes | **COOK TIME:** 8 hours

- **6 serving-sized pieces beef short ribs (about 3 pounds)**
- **2 tablespoons packed brown sugar**
- **3 cloves garlic, minced**
- **1 teaspoon dried thyme leaves, crushed**
- **¼ cup all-purpose flour**
- **1 can (10½ ounces) Campbell's® Condensed French Onion Soup**
- **1 bottle (12 fluid ounces) dark ale *or* beer**
- **Hot mashed potatoes *or* egg noodles**

1. Place the beef into a 5-quart slow cooker. Add the brown sugar, garlic, thyme and flour and toss to coat.

2. Stir the soup and ale in a small bowl. Pour over the beef.

3. Cover and cook on LOW for 8 to 9 hours* or until the beef is fork-tender. Serve with the mashed potatoes.

Or on HIGH for 4 to 5 hours.

Golden Chicken with Noodles

MAKES 8 SERVINGS | PREP TIME: 5 minutes | COOK TIME: 7 hours

2 cans (10¾ ounces *each*) Campbell's® Condensed Cream of Chicken Soup (Regular *or* 98% Fat Free)

½ cup water

¼ cup lemon juice

1 tablespoon Dijon-style mustard

1½ teaspoons garlic powder

8 large carrots, thickly sliced (about 6 cups)

8 skinless, boneless chicken breast halves

½ of a 12-ounce package egg noodles (about 4 cups), cooked and drained

Chopped fresh parsley

1. Stir the soup, water, lemon juice, mustard, garlic powder and carrots in a 3½-quart slow cooker. Add the chicken and turn to coat.

2. Cover and cook on LOW for 7 to 8 hours* or until the chicken is cooked through. Serve with the noodles. Sprinkle with the parsley.

Or on HIGH for 4 to 5 hours.

Slow-Cooked Pulled Pork Sandwiches

MAKES 12 SANDWICHES

PREP TIME: 15 minutes | COOK TIME: 8 hours | STAND TIME: 10 minutes

 1 **tablespoon vegetable oil**
 1 **(3½- to 4-pound) boneless pork shoulder roast, netted *or* tied**
 1 **can (10½ ounces) Campbell's® Condensed French Onion Soup**
 1 **cup ketchup**
 ¼ **cup cider vinegar**
 3 **tablespoons packed brown sugar**
12 **round sandwich rolls, split**

1. Heat the oil in a 10-inch skillet over medium-high heat. Add the roast and cook until it's well browned on all sides.

2. Stir the soup, ketchup, vinegar and brown sugar in a 5-quart slow cooker. Add the roast and turn to coat with the soup mixture.

3. Cover and cook on LOW for 8 to 10 hours* or until the meat is fork-tender.

4. Remove the roast from the cooker to a cutting board and let it stand for 10 minutes. Using 2 forks, shred the pork. Return the shredded pork to the cooker.

5. Divide the pork and sauce mixture among the rolls.

Or on HIGH for 4 to 5 hours.

Creamy Chicken Tortilla Soup

MAKES 4 SERVINGS | PREP TIME: 10 minutes | COOK TIME: 4 hours, 30 minutes

- **1 small red pepper, chopped (about ½ cup)**
- **1 small tomato, diced (about ½ cup)**
- **1 can (8¾ ounces) whole kernel corn, drained**
- **½ pound skinless, boneless chicken breasts, cut into ½-inch pieces**
- **1 can (10¾ ounces) Campbell's® Condensed Cream of Chicken Soup (Regular *or* 98% Fat Free)**
- **1½ cups water**
- **1 teaspoon ground cumin**
- **½ teaspoon ground coriander**
- **½ teaspoon garlic powder**
- **½ teaspoon chili powder**
- **1 can (about 4 ounces) chopped green chiles**
- **¼ teaspoon chopped jalapeño pepper (optional)**
- **2 corn tortillas (6-inch), cut into strips**
- **½ cup shredded Cheddar cheese**
- **¼ cup chopped fresh cilantro leaves**

1. Stir the pepper, tomato, corn and chicken in a 3½-quart slow cooker.

2. Stir the soup, water, cumin, coriander, garlic powder, chili powder, chiles and jalapeño pepper, if desired, in a small bowl. Pour over the chicken mixture.

3. Cover and cook on LOW for 4 to 5 hours* or until the chicken is cooked through.

4. Stir in the tortillas, cheese and cilantro. Cover and cook for 30 minutes. Serve with additional cheese, if desired.

Or on HIGH for 2 to 2½ hours.

Slow-Cooked Taco Shredded Beef

MAKES 16 TACOS

PREP TIME: 10 minutes | COOK TIME: 6 hours | STAND TIME: 10 minutes

  1 **can (10¾ ounces) Campbell's® Condensed French Onion Soup**
  1 **tablespoon chili powder**
  ½ **teaspoon ground cumin**
      2-pound boneless beef chuck roast
  2 **tablespoons finely chopped fresh cilantro leaves**
 16 **taco shells**
  1 **cup shredded Cheddar cheese (about 4 ounces)**
      Shredded lettuce
      Sour cream

1. Stir the soup, chili powder and cumin in a 4-quart slow cooker. Add the beef and turn to coat.

2. Cover and cook on LOW for 6 to 7 hours* or until the beef is fork-tender.

3. Remove the beef from the cooker to a cutting board and let stand for 10 minutes. Using 2 forks, shred the beef. Return the beef to the cooker. Stir the cilantro in the cooker.

4. Spoon **about ¼ cup** beef mixture into **each** taco shell. Top **each** with **about 1 tablespoon** cheese. Top with the lettuce and the sour cream.

Or on HIGH for 4 to 5 hours.

Slow-Cooked Autumn Brisket

MAKES 8 SERVINGS │ PREP TIME: 20 minutes │ COOK TIME: 8 hours

3-pound boneless beef brisket

1 **small head cabbage (about 1 pound), cut into 8 wedges**

1 **large sweet potato (about ¾ pound), peeled and cut into 1-inch pieces**

1 **large onion, cut into 8 wedges**

1 **medium Granny Smith apple, cored and cut into 8 wedges**

2 **cans (10¾ ounces *each*) Campbell's® Condensed Cream of Celery Soup (Regular *or* 98% Fat Free)**

1 **cup water**

2 **teaspoons caraway seed (optional)**

1. Place the brisket into a 6-quart slow cooker. Top with the cabbage, sweet potato, onion and apple. Stir the soup, water and caraway seed, if desired, in a small bowl. Pour the soup mixture over the brisket and vegetable mixture.

2. Cover and cook on LOW for 8 to 9 hours* or until the brisket is fork-tender. Season as desired.

Or on HIGH for 4 to 5 hours.

Chicken in Creamy Sun-Dried Tomato Sauce

MAKES 8 SERVINGS | **PREP TIME:** 15 minutes | **COOK TIME:** 7 hours

- **2 cans (10¾ ounces *each*) Campbell's® Condensed Cream of Chicken with Herbs Soup *or* Campbell's® Condensed Cream of Chicken Soup (Regular *or* 98% Fat Free)**
- **1 cup Chablis *or* other dry white wine**
- **¼ cup coarsely chopped pitted kalamata *or* oil-cured olives**
- **2 tablespoons drained capers**
- **2 cloves garlic, minced**
- **1 can (14 ounces) artichoke hearts, drained and chopped**
- **1 cup drained, coarsely chopped sun-dried tomatoes**
- **8 skinless, boneless chicken breast halves (about 2 pounds)**
- **½ cup chopped fresh basil leaves (optional)**
  Hot cooked rice, egg noodles *or* mashed potatoes

1. Stir the soup, wine, olives, capers, garlic, artichokes and tomatoes in a 3½-quart slow cooker. Add the chicken and turn to coat.

2. Cover and cook on LOW for 7 to 8 hours* or until the chicken is cooked through. Sprinkle with the basil, if desired. Serve with the rice.

Or on HIGH for 4 to 5 hours.

Kitchen Tip

*You can substitute **Swanson®** Chicken Broth for the wine, if desired.*

Slow Cooker Tuscan Beef Stew

MAKES 8 SERVINGS │ PREP TIME: 15 minutes │ COOK TIME: 8 hours, 10 minutes

- **1 can (10¾ ounces) Campbell's® Condensed Tomato Soup (Regular or Healthy Request®)**
- **1 can (10½ ounces) Campbell's® Condensed Beef Broth**
- **½ cup Burgundy wine or other dry red wine or water**
- **1 teaspoon dried Italian seasoning, crushed**
- **½ teaspoon garlic powder**
- **1 can (about 14.5 ounces) diced tomatoes with Italian herbs**
- **3 large carrots, cut into 1-inch pieces (about 2 cups)**
- **2 pounds beef for stew, cut into 1-inch pieces**
- **2 cans (about 16 ounces each) white kidney beans (cannellini), rinsed and drained**

1. Stir the soup, broth, wine, Italian seasoning, garlic powder, tomatoes, carrots and beef in a 3½-quart slow cooker.

2. Cover and cook on LOW for 8 to 9 hours* or until the beef is fork-tender.

3. Stir in the beans. Turn the heat to HIGH. Cook for 10 minutes or until the mixture is hot.

Or on HIGH for 4 to 5 hours.

Slow Cooker Savory Pot Roast

MAKES 6 SERVINGS | PREP TIME: 10 minutes | COOK TIME: 8 hours

1 **can (10¾ ounces) Campbell's® Condensed Cream of Mushroom Soup (Regular _or_ 98% Fat Free)**

1 **pouch (1 ounce) dry onion soup & recipe mix**

6 **small red potatoes, cut in half**

6 **medium carrots, cut into 2-inch pieces (about 3 cups)**

   3- to 3½-pound boneless beef bottom round roast _or_ chuck pot roast

1. Stir the soup, onion soup mix, potatoes and carrots in a 4½-quart slow cooker. Add the beef and turn to coat.

2. Cover and cook on LOW for 8 to 9 hours* or until the beef is fork-tender.

Or on HIGH for 4 to 5 hours.

Coq Au Vin

MAKES 6 SERVINGS | PREP TIME: 10 minutes | COOK TIME: 8 hours

- **1 package (10 ounces) sliced mushrooms**
- **1 bag (16 ounces) frozen whole small white onions**
- **1 sprig fresh rosemary leaves**
- **2 pounds skinless, boneless chicken thighs *and/or* breasts, cut into 1-inch strips**
- **¼ cup cornstarch**
- **1 can (10¾ ounces) Campbell's® Condensed Golden Mushroom Soup**
- **1 cup Burgundy *or* other dry red wine**
- **Hot mashed *or* oven-roasted potatoes**

1. Place the mushrooms, onions, rosemary and chicken into a 3½-quart slow cooker.

2. Stir the cornstarch, soup and wine in a small bowl. Pour over the chicken and vegetables.

3. Cover and cook on LOW for 8 to 9 hours*. Remove the rosemary. Serve with the mashed potatoes.

Or on HIGH for 4 to 5 hours.

satisfying sides

Greek Rice Bake

MAKES 6 SERVINGS

PREP TIME: 15 minutes | **BAKE TIME:** 40 minutes | **STAND TIME:** 5 minutes

- **1 can (10¾ ounces) Campbell's® Condensed Cream of Mushroom Soup (Regular _or_ 98% Fat Free)**
- **½ cup water**
- **1 can (about 14.5 ounces) diced tomatoes, undrained**
- **1 jar (6 ounces) marinated artichoke hearts, drained and cut in half**
- **2 portobello mushrooms, coarsely chopped (about 2 cups)**
- **¾ cup _uncooked_ quick-cooking brown rice**
- **1 can (about 15 ounces) small white beans, rinsed and drained**
- **3 to 4 tablespoons crumbled feta cheese**

1. Heat the oven to 400°F. Stir the soup, water, tomatoes, artichokes, mushrooms, rice and beans in a 2-quart casserole. Cover the casserole.

2. Bake for 40 minutes or until the rice is tender. Stir the rice mixture. Let stand for 5 minutes. Sprinkle with the cheese before serving.

Kitchen Tip

Different brands of quick-cooking brown rice cook differently, so the bake time for this recipe may be slightly longer or shorter than indicated.

Oven-Baked Risotto

MAKES 6 SERVINGS

PREP TIME: 15 minutes | **BAKE TIME:** 40 minutes | **STAND TIME:** 5 minutes

- 1 cup *uncooked* Arborio *or* regular long-grain white rice
- 1 can (10¾ ounces) Campbell's® Condensed Cream of Mushroom with Roasted Garlic Soup
- 1½ cups water
- 1 cup milk
- ¼ cup grated Parmesan cheese
- 2 tablespoons drained chopped sun-dried tomatoes
- 2 tablespoons chopped fresh parsley

1. Heat the oven to 400°F. Stir the rice, soup, water, milk, cheese and tomatoes in a 2-quart shallow baking dish. Cover the baking dish.

2. Bake for 30 minutes. Uncover the baking dish and stir the rice mixture. Bake, uncovered, for 10 minutes or until the rice is tender. Let stand for 5 minutes. Sprinkle with the parsley.

Kitchen Tip

*Add ½ **cup** frozen peas to the rice mixture before baking.*

Toasted Corn & Sage Harvest Risotto

MAKES 6 SERVINGS | **PREP TIME:** 15 minutes | **COOK TIME:** 35 minutes

- 1 tablespoon olive oil
- 1 cup fresh *or* drained canned whole kernel corn
- 1 large orange *or* red pepper, chopped (about 1 cup)
- 1 medium onion, chopped (about ½ cup)
- 1¾ cups *uncooked* regular long-grain white rice
- 4 cups Swanson® Chicken Broth (Regular, Natural Goodness® *or* Certified Organic)
- 1 teaspoon ground sage
- 1 can (10¾ ounces) Campbell's® Condensed Cream of Celery Soup (Regular *or* 98% Fat Free)
- ¼ cup grated Parmesan cheese

1. Heat the oil in a 4-quart saucepan over medium heat. Add the corn, pepper and onion and cook for 5 minutes or until the vegetables are lightly browned.

2. Add the rice to the saucepan and cook and stir for 30 seconds. Stir in the broth and sage and heat to a boil. Reduce the heat to low. Cover and cook for 20 minutes or until the rice is tender.

3. Stir in the soup. Cook for 2 minutes or until the rice mixture is hot. Sprinkle with the cheese.

Kitchen Tip

*If you want a meatless side dish, substitute **Swanson**® Vegetable Broth (Regular **or** Certified Organic) for the Chicken Broth.*

Cheesy Chile Corn Casserole

MAKES 6 SERVINGS | **PREP TIME:** 15 minutes | **BAKE TIME:** 30 minutes

- **1 can (10¾ ounces) Campbell's® Condensed Cheddar Cheese Soup**
- **¼ cup milk**
- **1 tablespoon butter, melted**
  Dash ground red pepper
- **1 bag (16 ounces) frozen whole kernel corn, thawed**
- **1 can (about 4 ounces) chopped green chiles**
- **1 can (2.8 ounces) French fried onions (about 1⅓ cups)**

1. Heat the oven to 350°F. Stir the soup, milk, butter, pepper, corn, chiles and ⅔ **cup** onions in a 1½-quart casserole.

2. Bake for 25 minutes or until the corn mixture is hot and bubbling. Stir the corn mixture.

3. Sprinkle the remaining onions over the corn mixture. Bake for 5 minutes or until the onions are golden brown.

Kitchen Tip

An oven thermometer is the best way to check how accurately your oven heats. Most are designed to hang on the rack inside your oven to conveniently measure the oven temperature.

Savory Mushroom Bread Pudding

MAKES 6 SERVINGS

PREP TIME: 5 minutes | **STAND TIME:** 30 minutes | **BAKE TIME:** 45 minutes

Vegetable cooking spray

12 slices Pepperidge Farm® White Sandwich Bread *or* Pepperidge Farm® Whole Grain 100% Whole Wheat Bread, cut into cubes

1 package (8 ounces) sliced mushrooms

1 can (10¾ ounces) Campbell's® Condensed Cream of Mushroom Soup (Regular *or* 98% Fat Free)

4 eggs

2½ cups milk

1 teaspoon dried thyme leaves, crushed

⅛ teaspoon ground black pepper

1 cup shredded Swiss cheese (about 4 ounces)

1. Heat the oven to 375°F. Spray a 13×9-inch (3-quart) shallow baking dish with cooking spray.

2. Add the bread and mushrooms to prepared baking dish.

3. Beat the soup, eggs, milk, thyme and black pepper with a whisk or a fork in a medium bowl. Pour over the bread and mushrooms, pressing down the bread to coat. Let stand for 30 minutes.

4. Bake for 35 minutes. Top with the cheese. Bake for 10 minutes more or until the cheese melts.

Green Bean Casserole

| MAKES 12 SERVINGS | PREP TIME: 10 minutes | BAKE TIME: 30 minutes |

- **2 cans (10¾ ounces *each*) Campbell's® Condensed Cream of Mushroom Soup (Regular *or* 98% Fat Free)**
- **1 cup milk**
- **2 teaspoons soy sauce**
- **¼ teaspoon ground black pepper**
- **2 bags (about 16 ounces *each*) frozen cut green beans, cooked and drained**
- **1 can (6 ounces) French fried onions (2⅔ cups)**

1. Stir the soup, milk, soy, black pepper, beans and **1⅓ cups** onions in a 3-quart casserole.

2. Bake at 350°F. for 25 minutes or until the bean mixture is hot and bubbling. Stir the bean mixture and top with the remaining onions.

3. Bake for 5 minutes or until the onions are golden brown.

Squash Casserole

MAKES 8 SERVINGS | **PREP TIME:** 15 minutes | **COOK TIME:** 40 minutes

- 3 cups Pepperidge Farm® Cornbread Stuffing
- ¼ cup butter *or* margarine, melted
- 1 can (10¾ ounces) Campbell's® Condensed Cream of Chicken Soup (Regular *or* 98% Fat Free)
- ½ cup sour cream
- 2 small yellow squash, shredded
- 2 small zucchini, shredded
- ¼ cup shredded carrot
- ½ cup shredded Cheddar cheese

1. Stir the stuffing and butter in a large bowl. Reserve ½ **cup** of the stuffing mixture and spoon remaining into a 2-quart shallow baking dish.

2. Stir the soup, sour cream, yellow squash, zucchini, carrot and cheese in a medium bowl. Spread the mixture over the stuffing mixture and sprinkle with the reserved stuffing mixture.

3. Bake at 350°F. for 40 minutes or until hot.

Creamy Souper Rice

MAKES 4 SERVINGS

PREP TIME: 5 minutes | **COOK TIME:** 10 minutes | **STAND TIME:** 5 minutes

- 1 can (10¾ ounces) Campbell's® Condensed Cream of Mushroom Soup (Regular *or* 98% Fat Free)
- 1½ cups Swanson® Natural Goodness® Chicken Broth
- 1½ cups *uncooked* instant white rice
- 1 tablespoon grated Parmesan cheese
  Freshly ground black pepper

1. Heat the soup and broth in a 2-quart saucepan over medium heat to a boil.

2. Stir the rice and cheese in the saucepan. Cover the saucepan and remove from the heat. Let stand for 5 minutes. Fluff the rice with a fork. Serve with the black pepper and additional Parmesan cheese.

Kitchen Tip

*Any of **Campbell's®** Condensed Cream Soups will work in this recipe: Cream of Chicken, Cream of Celery, even Cheddar Cheese.*

VOLUME MEASUREMENTS (dry)

1/8 teaspoon = 0.5 mL
1/4 teaspoon = 1 mL
1/2 teaspoon = 2 mL
3/4 teaspoon = 4 mL
1 teaspoon = 5 mL
1 tablespoon = 15 mL
2 tablespoons = 30 mL
1/4 cup = 60 mL
1/3 cup = 75 mL
1/2 cup = 125 mL
2/3 cup = 150 mL
3/4 cup = 175 mL
1 cup = 250 mL
2 cups = 1 pint = 500 mL
3 cups = 750 mL
4 cups = 1 quart = 1 L

VOLUME MEASUREMENTS (fluid)

1 fluid ounce (2 tablespoons) = 30 mL
4 fluid ounces (1/2 cup) = 125 mL
8 fluid ounces (1 cup) = 250 mL
12 fluid ounces (1 1/2 cups) = 375 mL
16 fluid ounces (2 cups) = 500 mL

WEIGHTS (mass)

1/2 ounce = 15 g
1 ounce = 30 g
3 ounces = 90 g
4 ounces = 120 g
8 ounces = 225 g
10 ounces = 285 g
12 ounces = 360 g
16 ounces = 1 pound = 450 g

DIMENSIONS

1/16 inch = 2 mm
1/8 inch = 3 mm
1/4 inch = 6 mm
1/2 inch = 1.5 cm
3/4 inch = 2 cm
1 inch = 2.5 cm

OVEN TEMPERATURES

250°F = 120°C
275°F = 140°C
300°F = 150°C
325°F = 160°C
350°F = 180°C
375°F = 190°C
400°F = 200°C
425°F = 220°C
450°F = 230°C

BAKING PAN AND DISH EQUIVALENTS

Utensil	Size in Inches	Size in Centimeters	Volume	Metric Volume
Baking or Cake Pan (square or rectangular)	8×8×2	20×20×5	8 cups	2 L
	9×9×2	23×23×5	10 cups	2.5 L
	13×9×2	33×23×5	12 cups	3 L
Loaf Pan	8½×4½×2½	21×11×6	6 cups	1.5 L
	9×9×3	23×13×7	8 cups	2 L
Round Layer Cake Pan	8×1½	20×4	4 cups	1 L
	9×1½	23×4	5 cups	1.25 L
Pie Plate	8×1½	20×4	4 cups	1 L
	9×1½	23×4	5 cups	1.25 L
Baking Dish or Casserole			1 quart/4 cups	1 L
			1½ quart/6 cups	1.5 L
			2 quart/8 cups	2 L
			3 quart/12 cups	3 L

Meatloaf

3. Heat **2 tablespoons** pan drippings, remaining soup and water in a 1-quart saucepan over medium heat until the mixture is hot and bubbling. Serve the sauce with the meatloaf.

Meatloaf Wellington: Prepare as above but bake loaf only 1 hour. Spoon off fat. Separate **1 package** (8 ounces) refrigerated crescent rolls. Place triangles crosswise over top and down sides of meatloaf, overlapping slightly. Bake 15 minutes more until golden.

Frosted Meatloaf: Prepare as above but bake loaf only 1 hour. Spoon off fat. Spread **3 cups** hot, seasoned mashed potatoes over loaf; sprinkle with ½ **cup** shredded Cheddar cheese. Bake 15 to 30 minutes more until meat is done.

Skillet Fiesta Chicken & Rice

Creamy Pork Marsala with Fettuccine

Skillet Fiesta Chicken & Rice

MAKES 4 SERVINGS | PREP TIME: 5 minutes | COOK TIME: 20 minutes

- **1 tablespoon vegetable oil**
- **4 skinless, boneless chicken breast halves**
- **1 can (10¾ ounces) Campbell's® Condensed Tomato Soup (Regular *or* Healthy Request®)**
- **1⅓ cups water**
- **1 teaspoon chili powder**
- **1½ cups *uncooked* instant white rice**
- **¼ cup shredded Cheddar cheese**

1. Heat the oil in a 10-inch skillet over medium-high heat. Add the chicken and cook for 10 minutes or until it's well browned on both sides. Remove the chicken from the skillet.

2. Stir the soup, water and chili powder in the skillet and heat to a boil.

3. Stir in the rice. Place the chicken on the rice mixture. Sprinkle the chicken with additional chili powder and the cheese. Reduce the heat to low. Cover and cook for 5 minutes or until the chicken is cooked through and the rice is tender. Stir the rice mixture before serving.

Kitchen Tip

Try Mexican-blend shredded cheese instead of the Cheddar if you like.

Creamy Pork Marsala with Fettuccine

MAKES 4 SERVINGS | PREP TIME: 5 minutes | COOK TIME: 25 minutes

- **1 tablespoon olive oil**
- **4 boneless pork chops, ¾-inch thick**
- **1 cup sliced mushrooms (about 3 ounces)**
- **1 clove garlic, minced**
- **1 can (10¾ ounces) Campbell's® Condensed Cream of Mushroom Soup (Regular *or* 98% Fat Free)**
- **½ cup milk**
- **2 tablespoons dry Marsala wine**
- **8 ounces spinach fettuccine, cooked and drained**

1. Heat the oil in a 10-inch skillet over medium-high heat. Add the pork and cook until it's well browned on both sides.

2. Reduce the heat to medium. Add the mushrooms and garlic to the skillet and cook until the mushrooms are tender.

3. Stir the soup, milk and wine in the skillet and heat to a boil. Reduce the heat to low. Cover and cook for 5 minutes or until the pork is cooked through. Serve the pork and sauce with the pasta.

Kitchen Tip

Marsalas can range from dry to sweet, so be sure to use a dry one for this recipe.

Simple Salisbury Steaks

French Onion Burgers

Simple Salisbury Steaks

MAKES 4 SERVINGS | PREP TIME: 15 minutes | COOK TIME: 25 minutes

- **1 can (10¾ ounces) Campbell's® Condensed Cream of Mushroom Soup (Regular *or* 98% Fat Free)**
- **1 pound ground beef**
- **⅓ cup dry bread crumbs**
- **1 small onion, finely chopped (about ¼ cup)**
- **1 egg, beaten**
- **1 tablespoon vegetable oil**
- **1½ cups sliced mushrooms (about 4 ounces)**

1. Thoroughly mix ¼ **cup** soup, beef, bread crumbs, onion and egg in a large bowl. Shape **firmly** into **4** (½-inch-thick) patties.

2. Heat the oil in a 10-inch skillet over medium-high heat. Add the patties and cook until they're well browned on both sides. Pour off any fat.

3. Add the remaining soup and mushrooms to the skillet and heat to a boil. Reduce the heat to low. Cover and cook for 10 minutes or until the patties are cooked through.

French Onion Burgers

MAKES 4 SERVINGS | PREP TIME: 5 minutes | COOK TIME: 20 minutes

- **1 pound ground beef**
- **1 can (10½ ounces) Campbell's® Condensed French Onion Soup**
- **4 slices Swiss cheese**
- **4 round hard rolls, split**

1. Shape the beef into **4** (½-inch-thick) burgers.

2. Heat a 10-inch skillet over medium-high heat. Add the burgers and cook until they're well browned on both sides. Remove the burgers from the skillet. Pour off any fat.

3. Stir the soup in the skillet and heat to a boil. Return the burgers to the skillet. Reduce the heat to low. Cover and cook for 5 minutes or until the burgers are cooked through. Top the burgers with the cheese and cook until the cheese is melted. Serve the burgers in the rolls with the soup mixture.

Kitchen Tip

You can also serve these burgers in a bowl atop a mound of hot mashed potatoes, with some of the onion gravy poured over.

Creamy Pesto Chicke

& Bow Ties

5 minutes | COOK TIME: 15 minutes

the butter in a 10-inch skillet
edium-high heat. Add the chicken
ok until it's well browned, stirring

the soup, milk and pesto sauce into
illet. Heat to a boil. Reduce the
to low. Cover and cook over low for
utes or until the chicken is cooked
gh. Stir in the pasta. Cook until it's

Chicken Quesadillas & Fiesta Rice

Tasty 2-Step Chicken

Chicken Quesadillas & Fiesta Rice

MAKES 10 QUESADILLAS | PREP TIME: 5 minutes | COOK TIME: 15 minutes

Vegetable cooking spray

1 pound skinless, boneless chicken breasts, cubed

1 can (10¾ ounces) Campbell's® Condensed Cheddar Cheese Soup

½ cup Pace® Picante Sauce

10 flour tortillas (8-inch)

Fiesta Rice (recipe follows)

1. Heat the oven to 425°F.

2. Spray a 10-inch skillet with cooking spray. Heat over medium-high heat for 1 minute. Add the chicken and cook until it's well browned, stirring often.

3. Stir the soup and salsa into the skillet. Cook until the mixture is hot and bubbling, stirring occasionally.

4. Put the tortillas on 2 baking sheets. Top **half** of each tortilla with **about** ⅓ **cup** soup mixture to within ½ inch of the edge. Moisten the edge of each tortilla with water. Fold over and press edges together to seal.

5. Bake for 5 minutes or until the filling is hot. Serve with **Fiesta Rice**.

Fiesta Rice: Heat 1 can Campbell's® Condensed Chicken Broth, ½ **cup** water and ½ **cup** Pace® Picante Sauce in a 2-quart saucepan over high heat to a boil. Stir in **2 cups uncooked** instant white rice. Cover and remove from the heat. Let stand 5 minutes, and then fluff the rice with a fork.

Tasty 2-Step Chicken

MAKES 6 SERVINGS | PREP TIME: 5 minutes | COOK TIME: 20 minutes

1 tablespoon vegetable oil

4 skinless, boneless chicken breast halves

1 can (10¾ ounces) Campbell's® Condensed Cream of Mushroom Soup (Regular *or* 98% Fat Free)

½ cup water

1. Heat the oil in a 10-inch skillet over medium-high heat. Add the chicken and cook for 10 minutes or until it's browned. Set the chicken aside. Pour off any fat.

2. Stir the soup and water into the skillet. Heat to a boil. Return the chicken to the skillet and reduce the heat to low. Cover and cook for 5 minutes or until the chicken is cooked through.

Paprika Chicken with Sour Cream Gravy

Paprika Chicken with Sour Cream Gravy

MAKES 4 SERVINGS | PREP TIME: 10 minutes | COOK TIME: 20 minutes

- ½ cup all-purpose flour
- 2 teaspoons paprika
- 1 teaspoon garlic powder
- 1 teaspoon ground black pepper
- 1 teaspoon ground red pepper
- 4 skinless, boneless chicken breast halves
- ¼ cup butter
- 1 can (10¾ ounces) Campbell's® Condensed Cream of Chicken Soup (Regular *or* 98% Fat Free)
- 2 green onions, sliced (about ¼ cup)
- 1 container (8 ounces) sour cream

1. Stir the flour, paprika, garlic powder, black pepper and red pepper on a plate. Coat the chicken with the paprika mixture.

2. Heat the butter in a 10-inch skillet over medium-high heat. Cook the chicken for 10 minutes or until it's well browned on both sides. Remove the chicken from the skillet.

3. Stir the soup and green onions in the skillet and heat to a boil. Return the chicken to the skillet. Reduce the heat to low. Cover and cook for 5 minutes or until the chicken is cooked through. Stir in the sour cream.

Kitchen Tip

Serve with a rice blend, steamed cut green beans and carrot slices.

Beefy Pasta Skillet

Campbell's

Easy Chicken & Biscuits

Campbell's

Beefy Pasta Skillet

MAKES 4 SERVINGS | **PREP TIME:** 5 minutes | **COOK TIME:** 15 minutes

1 pound ground beef

1 medium onion, chopped
(about ½ cup)

1 can (10¾ ounces) Campbell's®
Condensed Tomato Soup
(Regular *or* Healthy Request®)

¼ cup water

1 tablespoon Worcestershire sauce

½ cup shredded Cheddar cheese

2 cups cooked corkscrew-shaped pasta
(rotini) *or* elbow pasta

1. Cook the beef and onion in a 10-inch skillet over medium-high heat until the beef is well browned, stirring often to separate the meat. Pour off any fat.

2. Stir the soup, water, Worcestershire, cheese and pasta in the skillet and cook until the mixture is hot and bubbling.

Easy Chicken & Biscuits

MAKES 5 SERVINGS | **PREP TIME:** 10 minutes | **BAKE TIME:** 30 minutes

1 can (10¾ ounces) Campbell's®
Condensed Cream of Celery Soup
(Regular *or* 98% Fat Free)

1 can (10¾ ounces) Campbell's®
Condensed Cream of Potato Soup

1 cup milk

¼ teaspoon dried thyme leaves,
crushed

¼ teaspoon ground black pepper

4 cups cooked cut-up vegetables*

2 cups cubed cooked chicken

1 package (about 7 ounces) refrigerated
buttermilk biscuits (10)

*Use a combination of broccoli flowerets,
cauliflower flowerets and carrots.*

1. Stir the soups, milk, thyme, black pepper, vegetables and chicken in a 13×9×2-inch shallow baking dish.

2. Bake at 400°F. for 15 minutes. Stir.

3. Cut each biscuit into quarters. Arrange cut biscuits over the chicken mixture.

4. Bake for 15 minutes more or until the biscuits are golden.

Campbell's

Tuscan Turkey & Beans

Campbell's

Tuscan Turkey & Beans

MAKES 4 SERVINGS | **PREP TIME:** 10 minutes | **COOK TIME:** 20 minutes

- 2 tablespoons olive *or* vegetable oil
- 4 turkey breast cutlets *or* slices (about 1 pound)
- 1 medium onion, chopped (about ½ cup)
- 2 cloves garlic, minced
- 1½ teaspoons dried Italian seasoning, crushed
- 1 can (about 14.5 ounces) diced tomatoes, undrained
- 1½ cups packed chopped fresh spinach leaves
- 1 can (10¾ ounces) Campbell's® Condensed Cream of Celery Soup (Regular *or* 98% Fat Free)
- ¼ teaspoon ground black pepper
- 1 can (about 16 ounces) white kidney beans (cannellini), rinsed and drained

Grated *or* shredded Parmesan cheese

1. Heat **1 tablespoon** of the oil in a large skillet over medium-high heat. Add the turkey in 2 batches and cook for 3 minutes or until it's lightly browned on both sides. Remove the turkey from the skillet and set aside.

2. Add the remaining oil to the skillet and heat over medium heat. Add the onion, garlic and Italian seasoning and cook until the onion is tender-crisp, stirring often.

3. Add the tomatoes and the spinach and cook just until the spinach is wilted, stirring occasionally. Add the soup, black pepper and beans. Heat to a boil. Return the turkey to the skillet. Reduce the heat to low. Cover and cook for 5 minutes or until the turkey is cooked through. Sprinkle with the cheese.

Creamy Chicken Florentine

Campbell's

Tuna & Pasta Cheddar Melt

Campbell's

Creamy Chicken Florentine

MAKES 4 SERVINGS | **PREP TIME:** 15 minutes | **BAKE TIME:** 40 minutes | **STAND TIME:** 5 minutes

1 can (10¾ ounces) Campbell's®
  Condensed Cream of Chicken Soup
  (Regular *or* 98% Fat Free)

1½ cups water

½ of a 20-ounce bag frozen cut-leaf
  spinach, thawed and well drained
  (about 3½ cups)

1 can (about 14.5 ounces) diced
  tomatoes with Italian herbs

1 pound skinless, boneless chicken
  breasts, cut into 1-inch cubes

2½ cups *uncooked* penne pasta

½ cup shredded mozzarella cheese

1. Heat the oven to 375°F. Stir the soup, water, spinach, tomatoes and chicken in a 3-quart shallow baking dish. Cover the baking dish.

2. Bake for 20 minutes. Cook the pasta according to the package directions and drain well in a colander. Uncover the baking dish and stir in the pasta.

3. Bake for 20 minutes or until the pasta mixture is hot and bubbling. Sprinkle with the cheese. Let stand for 5 minutes or until the cheese is melted.

Tuna & Pasta Cheddar Melt

MAKES 4 SERVINGS | **PREP TIME:** 10 minutes | **COOK TIME:** 15 minutes

1 can (10½ ounces) Campbell's®
  Condensed Chicken Broth

1 soup can water

½ of a 1-pound package *uncooked*
  corkscrew-shaped pasta
  (rotini) (about 3 cups)

1 can (10¾ ounces) Campbell's®
  Condensed Cream of Mushroom
  Soup (Regular *or* 98% Fat Free)

1 cup milk

1 can (about 6 ounces) tuna, drained
  and flaked

1 cup shredded Cheddar cheese
  (about 4 ounces)

2 tablespoons Italian-seasoned dry
  bread crumbs

2 teaspoons butter or margarine,
  melted

1. Heat the broth and the water to a boil over medium-high heat in a large skillet. Add the pasta and cook until it's just tender, stirring often. Do not drain.

2. Stir the soup, milk and tuna in the skillet. Top with the cheese. Mix the bread crumbs with the butter. Sprinkle on top. Heat through.

Hearty Sausage & Rice Casserole

Campbell's

Beef Stroganoff

Campbell's

Hearty Sausage & Rice Casserole

MAKES 6 SERVINGS | PREP TIME: 30 minutes | BAKE TIME: 1 hour

1 pound bulk pork sausage

1 package (8 ounces) sliced mushrooms

2 stalks celery, coarsely chopped (about 1 cup)

1 large red pepper, coarsely chopped (about 1 cup)

1 large onion, coarsely chopped (about 1 cup)

1 teaspoon dried thyme leaves, crushed

½ teaspoon dried marjoram leaves, crushed

1 box (6 ounces) seasoned long-grain and wild rice mix

1¾ cups Swanson® Chicken Stock

1 can (10¾ ounces) Campbell's® Condensed Cream of Mushroom Soup (Regular *or* 98% Fat Free)

1 cup shredded Cheddar cheese (about 4 ounces)

1. Cook the sausage in a 12-inch skillet over medium-high heat until it's well browned, stirring often to separate meat. Pour off any fat.

2. Add the mushrooms, celery, pepper, onion, thyme, marjoram and seasoning packet from the rice blend to the skillet and cook until the vegetables are tender-crisp.

3. Stir the sausage mixture, stock, soup, rice blend and ½ **cup** cheese in a 3-quart shallow baking dish. Cover the baking dish.

4. Bake at 375°F. for 1 hour or until the sausage is cooked through and the rice is tender. Stir the sausage mixture before serving. Sprinkle with the remaining cheese.

Beef Stroganoff

MAKES 4 SERVINGS | PREP TIME: 10 minutes | COOK TIME: 25 minutes

1 tablespoon vegetable oil

1 pound boneless beef sirloin steak *or* beef top round steak, ¾-inch thick, cut into thin strips

1 medium onion, chopped (about ½ cup)

1 can (10¾ ounces) Campbell's® Condensed Cream of Mushroom Soup (Regular *or* 98% Fat Free)

½ teaspoon paprika

⅓ cup sour cream *or* plain yogurt

4 cups hot cooked whole wheat *or* regular egg noodles

Chopped fresh parsley

1. Heat the oil in a 12-inch nonstick skillet over medium-high heat. Add the beef and cook until it's well browned, stirring often. Remove the beef from the skillet. Pour off any fat.

2. Reduce the heat to medium. Add the onion to the skillet and cook until it's tender.

3. Stir the soup and paprika in the skillet and heat to a boil. Stir in the sour cream. Return the beef to the skillet and cook until the mixture is hot and bubbling. Serve the beef mixture over the noodles. Sprinkle with the parsley.

Skillet Vegetable Lasagna

Campbell's

Hearty Chicken & Noodle Casserole

Campbell's

Skillet Vegetable Lasagna

MAKES 6 SERVINGS | **PREP TIME:** 10 minutes | **BAKE TIME:** 15 minutes

1¾ cups Swanson® Vegetable Broth (Regular *or* Certified Organic)

⅔ of a 1-pound package of *uncooked* oven-ready (no-boil) lasagna noodles (about 15)

1 can (10¾ ounces) Campbell's® Condensed Cream of Mushroom Soup (Regular *or* 98% Fat Free)

1 can (about 14.5 ounces) diced tomatoes, undrained

1 package (10 ounces) frozen chopped spinach, thawed and well drained

1 cup ricotta cheese

1 cup shredded mozzarella cheese (about 4 ounces)

1. Heat the broth in a 12-inch skillet over medium-high heat to a boil. Break the noodles into pieces and add to the broth. Reduce the heat to low. Cook for 3 minutes or until the noodles are tender.

2. Stir the soup, tomatoes and spinach in the skillet. Cook for 5 minutes or until the mixture is hot and bubbling.

3. Remove the skillet from the heat. Spoon the ricotta cheese on top and sprinkle with the mozzarella cheese.

Kitchen Tip

*You can try using **4 ounces** mozzarella, cut into very thin slices, instead of the shredded mozzarella.*

Hearty Chicken & Noodle Casserole

MAKES 4 SERVINGS | **PREP TIME:** 15 minutes | **BAKE TIME:** 25 minutes

1 can (10¾ ounces) Campbell's® Condensed Cream of Mushroom Soup (Regular *or* 98% Fat Free)

½ cup milk

¼ teaspoon ground black pepper

1 cup frozen mixed vegetables

2 cups cubed cooked chicken

¼ of a 12-ounce package medium egg noodles (about 2 cups), cooked and drained

¼ cup grated Parmesan cheese

½ cup shredded Cheddar cheese

1. Heat the oven to 400°F. Stir the soup, milk, black pepper, vegetables, chicken, noodles and Parmesan cheese in a 1½-quart casserole.

2. Bake for 25 minutes or until the chicken mixture is hot and bubbling. Stir the chicken mixture. Top with the Cheddar cheese.

Kitchen Tip

*Easy casseroles like this one are a simple way to transform leftovers; cooked chicken, turkey **or** ham will all work in this recipe. Or, substitute **1 can** (12.5 ounces) Swanson® Premium White Chunk Chicken Breast, drained, for the cubed cooked chicken.*

Chicken Broccoli Divan

One-Dish Chicken & Stuffing Bake

Chicken Broccoli Divan

MAKES 4 SERVINGS | **PREP TIME:** 10 minutes | **BAKE TIME:** 20 minutes

- 4 **cups cooked broccoli flowerets**
- 1½ **cups cubed cooked chicken**
- 1 **can (10¾ ounces) Campbell's®
  Condensed Cream of Chicken Soup
  (Regular *or* 98% Fat Free)**
- ⅓ **cup milk**
- ½ **cup shredded Cheddar cheese**
- 2 **tablespoons dry bread crumbs**
- 1 **tablespoon butter, melted**

1. Heat the oven to 450°F. Place the broccoli and chicken into a 9-inch deep-dish pie plate.

2. Stir the soup and milk in a small bowl. Pour the soup mixture over the broccoli and chicken. Sprinkle with the cheese. Stir the bread crumbs and butter in a small bowl. Sprinkle the bread crumbs over the cheese.

3. Bake for 20 minutes or until the cheese is melted and the bread crumbs are golden brown.

Kitchen Tip

You can use leftover cooked turkey instead of the chicken in this recipe.

One-Dish Chicken & Stuffing Bake

MAKES 6 SERVINGS | **PREP TIME:** 15 minutes | **COOK TIME:** 30 minutes

- 4 **cups Pepperidge Farm® Herb
  Seasoned Stuffing**
- 6 **skinless, boneless chicken breast
  halves**
  Paprika
- 1 **can (10¾ ounces) Campbell's®
  Condensed Cream of Mushroom
  Soup (Regular *or* 98% Fat Free)**
- ⅓ **cup milk**
- 1 **tablespoon chopped fresh parsley
  or 1 teaspoon dried parsley flakes**

1. Heat the oven to 400°F. Prepare the stuffing according to the package directions.

2. Spoon the stuffing across the center of a 3-quart shallow baking dish. Place the chicken on either side of the stuffing. Sprinkle the chicken with the paprika.

3. Stir the soup, milk and parsley in a small bowl. Pour the soup mixture over the chicken. Cover the baking dish.

4. Bake for 30 minutes or until the chicken is cooked through.

Kitchen Tip

***4 cups** of any variety of **Pepperidge Farm®**
Stuffing will work in this recipe.*

New Orleans Shrimp Toss

Beef Taco Skillet

New Orleans Shrimp Toss

MAKES 4 SERVINGS | **PREP TIME:** 15 minutes | **COOK TIME:** 10 minutes

1 **pound large shrimp, shelled and deveined**

2 **tablespoons vegetable oil**

2 **tablespoons lemon juice**

1 **tablespoon Worcestershire sauce**

1 **teaspoon Cajun seasoning**

½ **cup chopped onion**

2 **cloves garlic, chopped**

1 **can Campbell's® Condensed Cream of Chicken with Herbs Soup**

½ **cup milk**

1 **teaspoon paprika**

2 **tablespoons chopped fresh chives (optional)**

Cornbread *or* biscuits

1. Stir the shrimp, **1 tablespoon** oil, lemon juice, Worcestershire and Cajun seasoning in a medium bowl.

2. Heat the remaining oil in a 10-inch skillet over medium heat. Add the onion and garlic and cook until they're tender.

3. Stir the soup, milk and paprika in the skillet. Heat to a boil. Add the shrimp mixture. Reduce the heat to low. Cover and cook for 5 minutes or until the shrimp are done. Garnish with the chives, if desired. Serve with the cornbread.

Beef Taco Skillet

MAKES 4 SERVINGS | **PREP TIME:** 5 minutes | **COOK TIME:** 20 minutes

1 **pound ground beef**

1 **can (10¾ ounces) Campbell's® Condensed Tomato Soup (Regular *or* Healthy Request®)**

½ **cup salsa**

½ **cup water**

6 **flour tortillas (6-inch), cut into 1-inch pieces**

½ **cup shredded Cheddar cheese**

1. Cook the beef in a 10-inch skillet over medium-high heat until it's well browned, stirring often to separate meat. Pour off any fat.

2. Stir the soup, salsa, water and tortillas in the skillet and heat to a boil. Reduce the heat to low. Cook for 5 minutes. Stir the beef mixture. Top with the cheese.

Creamy Pork Sauté

Creamy Pork Sauté

MAKES 4 SERVINGS | **PREP TIME:** 10 minutes | **COOK TIME:** 25 minutes

- 2 tablespoons vegetable oil
- 1 pound boneless pork loin, cut into thin strips
- 2 stalks celery, sliced (about 1 cup)
- 1 medium onion, chopped (about ½ cup)
- ½ teaspoon dried thyme leaves, crushed
- 1 can (10¾ ounces) Campbell's® Condensed Cream of Celery Soup (Regular *or* 98% Fat Free)
- ¼ cup water
  Hot cooked regular long-grain white rice

1. Heat **1 tablespoon** oil in a 10-inch skillet over medium-high heat. Add the pork and cook until it's well browned, stirring often. Remove the pork from the skillet.

2. Heat the remaining oil over medium heat. Add the celery, onion and thyme and cook until the vegetables are tender, stirring often.

3. Stir the soup and water in the skillet and heat to a boil. Return the pork to the skillet. Cook until the pork is cooked through. Serve the pork mixture over the rice.

Slow-Cooked Pulled Pork Sandwiches

Slow-Cooked Pulled Pork Sandwiches

MAKES 12 SANDWICHES | PREP TIME: 15 minutes | COOK TIME: 8 hours | STAND TIME: 10 minutes

- 1 **tablespoon vegetable oil**
- 1 **(3½- to 4-pound) boneless pork shoulder roast, netted *or* tied**
- 1 **can (10½ ounces) Campbell's® Condensed French Onion Soup**
- 1 **cup ketchup**
- ¼ **cup cider vinegar**
- 3 **tablespoons packed brown sugar**
- 12 **round sandwich rolls, split**

1. Heat the oil in a 10-inch skillet over medium-high heat. Add the roast and cook until it's well browned on all sides.

2. Stir the soup, ketchup, vinegar and brown sugar in a 5-quart slow cooker. Add the roast and turn to coat with the soup mixture.

3. Cover and cook on LOW for 8 to 10 hours* or until the meat is fork-tender.

4. Remove the roast from the cooker to a cutting board and let it stand for 10 minutes. Using 2 forks, shred the pork. Return the shredded pork to the cooker.

5. Divide the pork and sauce mixture among the rolls.

Or on HIGH for 4 to 5 hours.

Chicken in Creamy Sun-Dried Tomato Sauce

Campbell's

Slow Cooker Tuscan Beef Stew

Campbell's

Chicken in Creamy Sun-Dried Tomato Sauce

MAKES 8 SERVINGS | PREP TIME: 15 minutes | COOK TIME: 7 hours

2 cans (10¾ ounces *each*) Campbell's® Condensed Cream of Chicken with Herbs Soup *or* Campbell's® Condensed Cream of Chicken Soup (Regular *or* 98% Fat Free)

1 cup Chablis *or* other dry white wine

¼ cup coarsely chopped pitted kalamata *or* oil-cured olives

2 tablespoons drained capers

2 cloves garlic, minced

1 can (14 ounces) artichoke hearts, drained and chopped

1 cup drained, coarsely chopped sun-dried tomatoes

8 skinless, boneless chicken breast halves (about 2 pounds)

½ cup chopped fresh basil leaves (optional)

Hot cooked rice, egg noodles *or* mashed potatoes

1. Stir the soup, wine, olives, capers, garlic, artichokes and tomatoes in a 3½-quart slow cooker. Add the chicken and turn to coat.

2. Cover and cook on LOW for 7 to 8 hours* or until the chicken is cooked through. Sprinkle with the basil, if desired. Serve with the rice.

Or on HIGH for 4 to 5 hours.

Kitchen Tip

You can substitute **Swanson®** *Chicken Broth for the wine, if desired.*

Slow Cooker Tuscan Beef Stew

MAKES 8 SERVINGS | PREP TIME: 15 minutes | COOK TIME: 8 hours, 10 minutes

1 can (10¾ ounces) Campbell's® Condensed Tomato Soup (Regular *or* Healthy Request®)

1 can (10½ ounces) Campbell's® Condensed Beef Broth

½ cup Burgundy wine *or* other dry red wine *or* water

1 teaspoon dried Italian seasoning, crushed

½ teaspoon garlic powder

1 can (about 14.5 ounces) diced tomatoes with Italian herbs

3 large carrots, cut into 1-inch pieces (about 2 cups)

2 pounds beef for stew, cut into 1-inch pieces

2 cans (about 16 ounces *each*) white kidney beans (cannellini), rinsed and drained

1. Stir the soup, broth, wine, Italian seasoning, garlic powder, tomatoes, carrots and beef in a 3½-quart slow cooker.

2. Cover and cook on LOW for 8 to 9 hours* or until the beef is fork-tender.

3. Stir in the beans. Turn the heat to HIGH. Cook for 10 minutes or until the mixture is hot.

Or on HIGH for 4 to 5 hours.

Slow Cooker Savory Pot Roast

Coq Au Vin

Slow Cooker Savory Pot Roast

MAKES 6 SERVINGS | PREP TIME: 10 minutes | COOK TIME: 8 hours

1 can (10¾ ounces) Campbell's® Condensed Cream of Mushroom Soup (Regular *or* 98% Fat Free)

1 pouch (1 ounce) dry onion soup & recipe mix

6 small red potatoes, cut in half

6 medium carrots, cut into 2-inch pieces (about 3 cups)

3- to 3½-pound boneless beef bottom round roast *or* chuck pot roast

1. Stir the soup, onion soup mix, potatoes and carrots in a 4½-quart slow cooker. Add the beef and turn to coat.

2. Cover and cook on LOW for 8 to 9 hours* or until the beef is fork-tender.

Or on HIGH for 4 to 5 hours.

Coq Au Vin

MAKES 6 SERVINGS | PREP TIME: 10 minutes | COOK TIME: 8 hours

1 package (10 ounces) sliced mushrooms

1 bag (16 ounces) frozen whole small white onions

1 sprig fresh rosemary leaves

2 pounds skinless, boneless chicken thighs *and/or* breasts, cut into 1-inch strips

¼ cup cornstarch

1 can (10¾ ounces) Campbell's® Condensed Golden Mushroom Soup

1 cup Burgundy *or* other dry red wine

Hot mashed *or* oven-roasted potatoes

1. Place the mushrooms, onions, rosemary and chicken into a 3½-quart slow cooker.

2. Stir the cornstarch, soup and wine in a small bowl. Pour over the chicken and vegetables.

3. Cover and cook on LOW for 8 to 9 hours*. Remove the rosemary. Serve with the mashed potatoes.

Or on HIGH for 4 to 5 hours.

Greek Rice Bake

Oven-Baked Risotto

Greek Rice Bake

MAKES 6 SERVINGS | PREP TIME: 15 minutes | **BAKE TIME:** 40 minutes | **STAND TIME:** 5 minutes

1 can (10¾ ounces) Campbell's®
   Condensed Cream of Mushroom
   Soup (Regular *or* 98% Fat Free)

½ cup water

1 can (about 14.5 ounces) diced
   tomatoes, undrained

1 jar (6 ounces) marinated artichoke
   hearts, drained and cut in half

2 portobello mushrooms, coarsely
   chopped (about 2 cups)

¾ cup *uncooked* quick-cooking brown
   rice

1 can (about 15 ounces) small white
   beans, rinsed and drained

3 to 4 tablespoons crumbled feta
   cheese

1. Heat the oven to 400°F. Stir the soup, water, tomatoes, artichokes, mushrooms, rice and beans in a 2-quart casserole. Cover the casserole.

2. Bake for 40 minutes or until the rice is tender. Stir the rice mixture. Let stand for 5 minutes. Sprinkle with the cheese before serving.

Kitchen Tip

Different brands of quick-cooking brown rice cook differently, so the bake time for this recipe may be slightly longer or shorter than indicated.

Oven-Baked Risotto

MAKES 6 SERVINGS | PREP TIME: 15 minutes | **BAKE TIME:** 40 minutes | **STAND TIME:** 5 minutes

1 cup *uncooked* Arborio *or* regular
   long-grain white rice

1 can (10¾ ounces) Campbell's®
   Condensed Cream of Mushroom
   with Roasted Garlic Soup

1½ cups water

1 cup milk

¼ cup grated Parmesan cheese

2 tablespoons drained chopped
   sun-dried tomatoes

2 tablespoons chopped fresh parsley

1. Heat the oven to 400°F. Stir the rice, soup, water, milk, cheese and tomatoes in a 2-quart shallow baking dish. Cover the baking dish.

2. Bake for 30 minutes. Uncover the baking dish and stir the rice mixture. Bake, uncovered, for 10 minutes or until the rice is tender. Let stand for 5 minutes. Sprinkle with the parsley.

Kitchen Tip

*Add ½ **cup** frozen peas to the rice mixture before baking.*

Toasted Corn & Sage Harvest Risotto

Campbell's

Toasted Corn & Sage Harvest Risotto

MAKES 6 SERVINGS | **PREP TIME:** 15 minutes | **COOK TIME:** 35 minutes

- 1 tablespoon olive oil
- 1 cup fresh *or* drained canned whole kernel corn
- 1 large orange *or* red pepper, chopped (about 1 cup)
- 1 medium onion, chopped (about ½ cup)
- 1¾ cups *uncooked* regular long-grain white rice
- 4 cups Swanson® Chicken Broth (Regular, Natural Goodness® *or* Certified Organic)
- 1 teaspoon ground sage
- 1 can (10¾ ounces) Campbell's® Condensed Cream of Celery Soup (Regular *or* 98% Fat Free)
- ¼ cup grated Parmesan cheese

1. Heat the oil in a 4-quart saucepan over medium heat. Add the corn, pepper and onion and cook for 5 minutes or until the vegetables are lightly browned.

2. Add the rice to the saucepan and cook and stir for 30 seconds. Stir in the broth and sage and heat to a boil. Reduce the heat to low. Cover and cook for 20 minutes or until the rice is tender.

3. Stir in the soup. Cook for 2 minutes or until the rice mixture is hot. Sprinkle with the cheese.

Kitchen Tip

*If you want a meatless side dish, substitute **Swanson®** Vegetable Broth (Regular **or** Certified Organic) for the Chicken Broth.*

Savory Mushroom Bread Pudding

Campbell's

Green Bean Casserole

Campbell's

Savory Mushroom Bread Pudding

MAKES 6 SERVINGS | **PREP TIME:** 5 minutes | **STAND TIME:** 30 minutes | **BAKE TIME:** 45 minutes

Vegetable cooking spray

12 slices Pepperidge Farm® White Sandwich Bread **or** Pepperidge Farm® Whole Grain 100% Whole Wheat Bread, cut into cubes

1 package (8 ounces) sliced mushrooms

1 can (10¾ ounces) Campbell's® Condensed Cream of Mushroom Soup (Regular **or** 98% Fat Free)

4 eggs

2½ cups milk

1 teaspoon dried thyme leaves, crushed

⅛ teaspoon ground black pepper

1 cup shredded Swiss cheese (about 4 ounces)

1. Heat the oven to 375°F. Spray a 13×9-inch (3-quart) shallow baking dish with cooking spray.

2. Add the bread and mushrooms to prepared baking dish.

3. Beat the soup, eggs, milk, thyme and black pepper with a whisk or a fork in a medium bowl. Pour over the bread and mushrooms, pressing down the bread to coat. Let stand for 30 minutes.

4. Bake for 35 minutes. Top with the cheese. Bake for 10 minutes more or until the cheese melts.

Green Bean Casserole

MAKES 12 SERVINGS | **PREP TIME:** 10 minutes | **BAKE TIME:** 30 minutes

2 cans (10¾ ounces **each**) Campbell's® Condensed Cream of Mushroom Soup (Regular **or** 98% Fat Free)

1 cup milk

2 teaspoons soy sauce

¼ teaspoon ground black pepper

2 bags (about 16 ounces **each**) frozen cut green beans, cooked and drained

1 can (6 ounces) French fried onions (2⅔ cups)

1. Stir the soup, milk, soy, black pepper, beans and 1⅓ **cups** onions in a 3-quart casserole.

2. Bake at 350°F. for 25 minutes or until the bean mixture is hot and bubbling. Stir the bean mixture and top with the remaining onions.

3. Bake for 5 minutes or until the onions are golden brown.

Squash Casserole

Creamy Souper Rice

Squash Casserole

MAKES 8 SERVINGS | **PREP TIME:** 15 minutes | **COOK TIME:** 40 minutes

3 cups Pepperidge Farm® Cornbread Stuffing

¼ cup butter *or* margarine, melted

1 can (10¾ ounces) Campbell's® Condensed Cream of Chicken Soup (Regular *or* 98% Fat Free)

½ cup sour cream

2 small yellow squash, shredded

2 small zucchini, shredded

¼ cup shredded carrot

½ cup shredded Cheddar cheese

1. Stir the stuffing and butter in a large bowl. Reserve ½ **cup** of the stuffing mixture and spoon remaining into a 2-quart shallow baking dish.

2. Stir the soup, sour cream, yellow squash, zucchini, carrot and cheese in a medium bowl. Spread the mixture over the stuffing mixture and sprinkle with the reserved stuffing mixture.

3. Bake at 350°F. for 40 minutes or until hot.

Creamy Souper Rice

MAKES 4 SERVINGS | **PREP TIME:** 5 minutes | **COOK TIME:** 10 minutes | **STAND TIME:** 5 minutes

1 can (10¾ ounces) Campbell's® Condensed Cream of Mushroom Soup (Regular *or* 98% Fat Free)

1½ cups Swanson® Natural Goodness® Chicken Broth

1½ cups *uncooked* instant white rice

1 tablespoon grated Parmesan cheese Freshly ground black pepper

1. Heat the soup and broth in a 2-quart saucepan over medium heat to a boil.

2. Stir the rice and cheese in the saucepan. Cover the saucepan and remove from the heat. Let stand for 5 minutes. Fluff the rice with a fork. Serve with the black pepper and additional Parmesan cheese.

Kitchen Tip

*Any of **Campbell's**® Condensed Cream Soups will work in this recipe: Cream of Chicken, Cream of Celery, even Cheddar Cheese.*